C000240959

Charlie Ellis

summersdale

SILLY DOGS

When you spot someone opening the office snacks.

SILLY DOGS

An Hachette UK Company
www.hachette.co.uk

Summersdale Publishers
Part of Octopus Publishing Group Limited
Carmelite House
50 Victoria Embankment
LONDON
EC4Y 0DZ
UK

www.summersdale.com

Printed and bound in China

ISBN: 978-1-83799-408-3

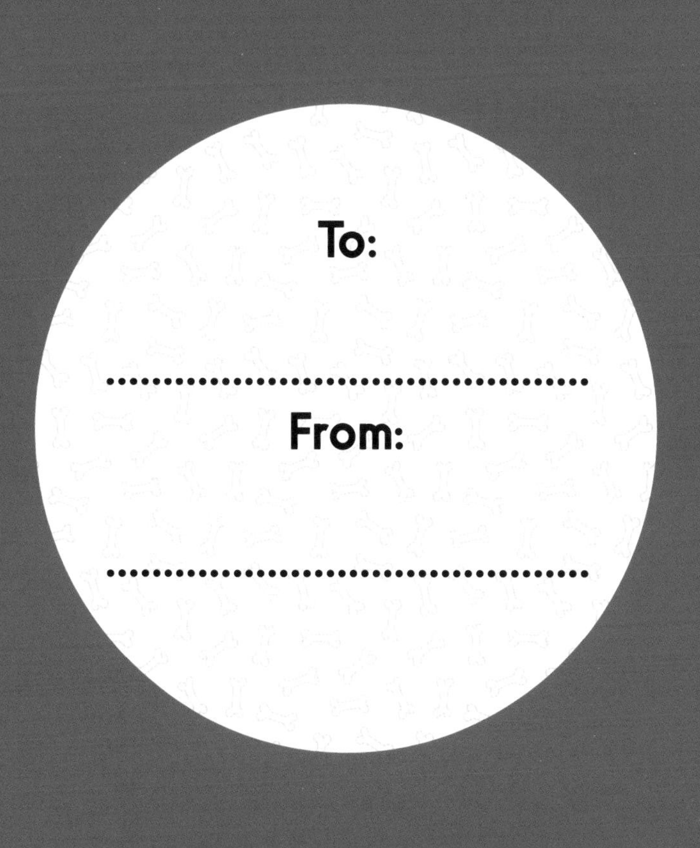
To:
From:

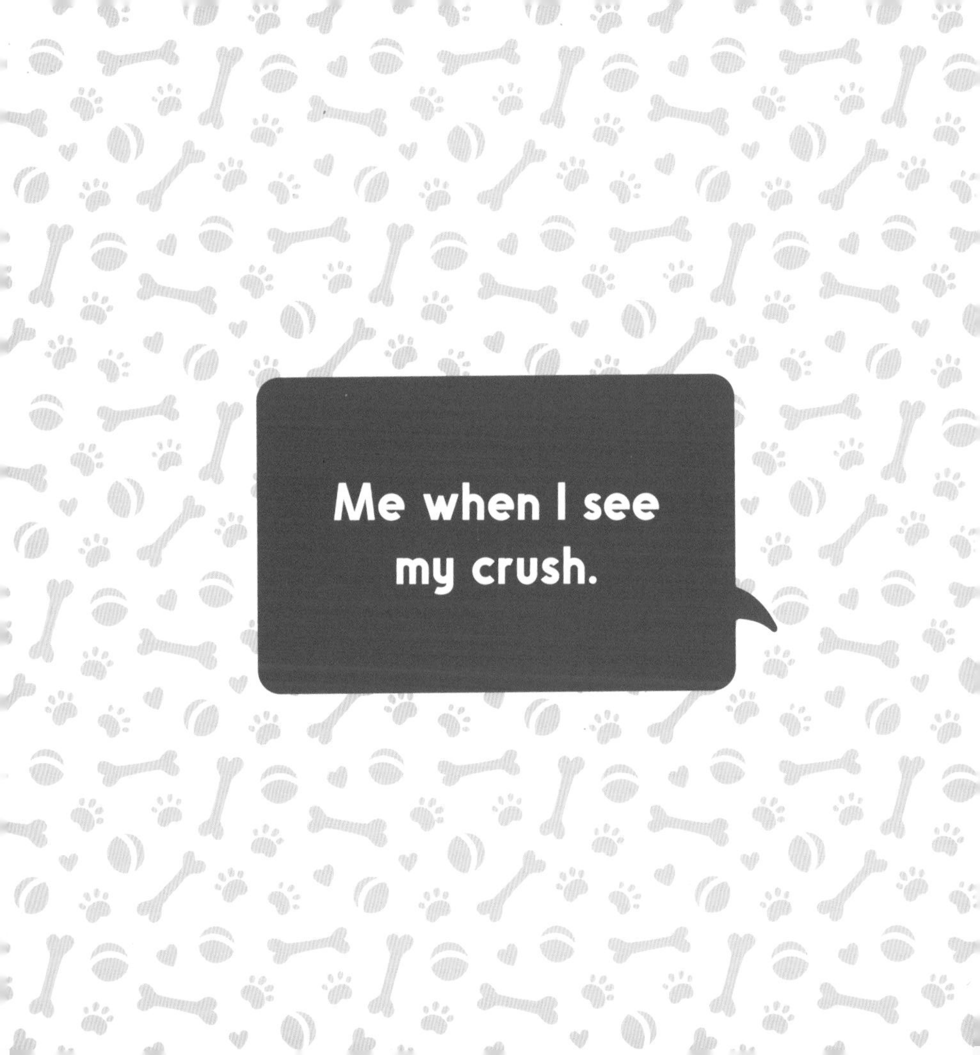
Me when I see
my crush.

ONE GiANT LEAP
FOR DOG-KiND.

"He's a ten but he doesn't believe in belly rubs."

ME STiCKiNG
MY HEAD UNDER
THE TAP AFTER
A NiGHT OUT.

When you randomly remember something embarrassing you did five years ago.

POV: you're a passenger princess.

CRiED BUT DiD THE
THiNG ANYWAY.

Monday, we
meet again.

When you have definitely not been at the snack cupboard.

Welcome to my crib.

When you accidentally
open your front camera.

NiCE CUSHiON. IT'D BE
A SHAME iF SOMEONE...
DESTROYED iT.

When you finish the washing up but notice you've left a pan on the hob.

WHEN YOU HAVEN'T GOT THE ENERGY TO HAKUNA OR MATATA.

Sliding into
those DMs like...

ME AT 8:59
WHEN I
HAVE WORK
AT 9:00.

Me: Don't look now, but...

My friend:

What, this?
It's vegan.

I'M JUST GONNA SCOOCH
iN RiGHT HERE.

Me when I
work out who the
murderer is before
the end of the
movie.

Me avoiding my responsibilities like...

Felt cute, might
delete later.

POV: your
doorbell camera.

WHEN I SAY I ALREADY HAVE PLANS, THiS iS WHAT I MEAN.

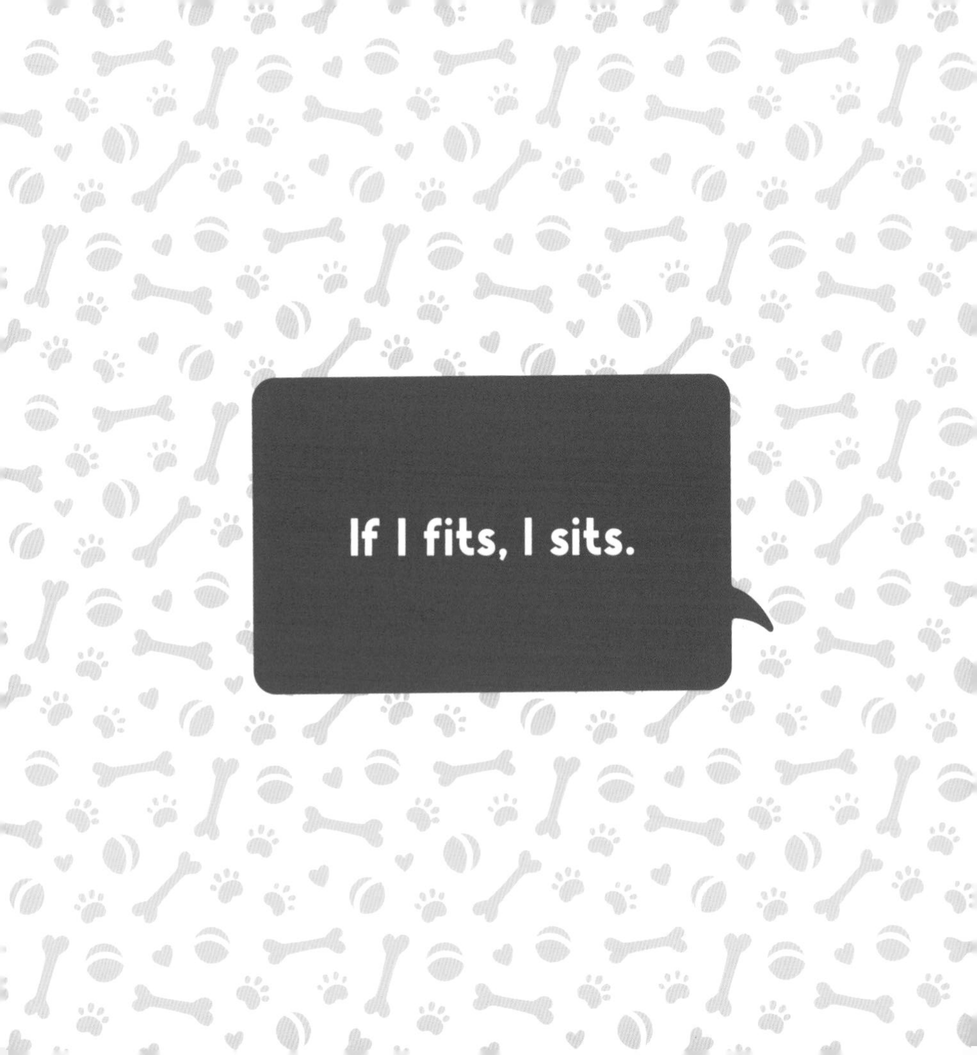
If I fits, I sits.

WHEN THOSE SHOWER
THOUGHTS HiT YOU.

It’s too late for me.
Save yourselves!

I JUST LOVE
SWEATER
WEATHER,
DON'T YOU?

When Mum says
dinner will be
5 minutes late.

Waiting for your morning coffee to kick in like...

POV: BEING WOKEN UP BY ME
ON CHRISTMAS MORNING.

Get in loser, we're going Shopping.

Just hanging out. Wbu?

Yeah, it's real –
stop staring.

All work and no play
makes Dog a dull boy.

THAT FEELiNG WHEN iT'S FiNALLY PUMPKiN SPiCE LATTE SEASON.

This is how the kids are wearing it.

ME WAITING FOR MY
WORK BESTIE TO GET BACK
FROM THEIR HOLIDAY.

They see me rollin'.

IT'S CALLED
FASHiON –
LOOK iT UP.

When it's
9:05 and
your owner's
not due back
until 5:00.

When you wake
up and forget what
planet you’re on.

WHEN YOU SPOT SOMEONE
OPENiNG THE OFFiCE SNACKS.

I love you so much I’m gonna eat you. Sorry, I don’t make the rules.

Him? He's my brother
from another mother.

SiLLY CATS

Charlie Ellis

Hardback

978-1-83799-406-9

Feline low? This hilarious collection of silly cats will lighten your mood and leave you laughing out meowed

Cats are packed with purrsonality, and this book celebrates exactly that. With their funny faces and bizarre body positions, the silly cats in this collection will entertain feline fanatics and animal whisperers alike.

Image credits

Cover image © smrm1977/Shutterstock.com; Back cover image © Master1305/Shutterstock.com; Paws © Omeris/Shutterstock.com; p.3 and throughout © CNuisin/Shutterstock.com; p.4 and throughout © Elena Pimukova/Shutterstock.com; p.5 © BCFC/Shutterstock.com; p.6 © Best dog photo/Shutterstock.com; p.8 and throughout © CNuisin/Shutterstock.com; p.9 © RavenaJuly/Shutterstock.com; p.10 © Tom Meaker/Shutterstock.com; p.13 © Konstantin Zaykov/Shutterstock.com; p.14 © anetapics/Shutterstock.com; p.17 © Phuttharak/Shutterstock.com; p.18 © B.Stefanov/Shutterstock.com; p.19 and throughout © Lili Kudrili/Shutterstock.com; p.21 © Cindy Hughes/Shutterstock.com; p.22 © Elina_KV/Shutterstock.com; p.24 and throughout © CNuisin/Shutterstock.com; p.25 © Annette Shaff/Shutterstock.com; p.26 © Zanna Pesnina/Shutterstock.com; p.29 © Crystal Alba/Shutterstock.com; p.30 © Sophia Cole/Shutterstock.com; p.33 © Rita_Kochmarjova/Shutterstock.com; p.34 © Soloviova Liudmyla/Shutterstock.com; p.37 © Tanya Dol/Shutterstock.com; p.38 © Jaromir Chalabala/Shutterstock.com; p.41 © Markik/Shutterstock.com; p.42 © Kamonporn wangjaroen/Shutterstock.com; p.45 © smrm1977/Shutterstock.com; p.46 © Kruzich/Shutterstock.com; p.49 © Annette Shaff/Shutterstock.com; p.50 © Vitaly Titov/Shutterstock.com; p.53 © New Africa/Shutterstock.com; p.54 © DeZPhoto/Shutterstock.com; p.57 © Igor Normann/Shutterstock.com; p.58 © Pixel-Shot/Shutterstock.com; p.61 © Paul's Lady/Shutterstock.com; p.62 © Camptoloma/Shutterstock.com; p.65 © Master1305/Shutterstock.com; p.66 © Tara Lynn and Co/Shutterstock.com; p.69 © Ksenia Raykova/Shutterstock.com; p.70 © Nan Liu/Shutterstock.com; p.73 © Monkey Business Images/Shutterstock.com; p.74 © GIOIA PHOTO/Shutterstock.com; p.77 © Happy monkey/Shutterstock.com; p.78 © Jaromir Chalabala/Shutterstock.com; p.81 © Denton Rumsey/Shutterstock.com; p.82 © otsphoto/Shutterstock.com; p.85 © Margarita Mindebaeva/Shutterstock.com; p.86 © Ermolaev Alexander/Shutterstock.com; p.89 © smrm1977/Shutterstock.com; p.90 © nancy dressel/Shutterstock.com; p.93 © Rita_Kochmarjova/Shutterstock.com

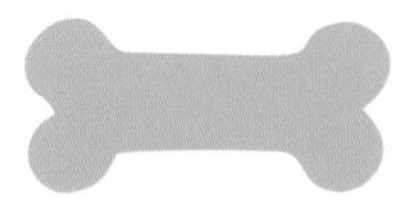

Have you enjoyed this book?
If so, find us on Facebook at **Summersdale Publishers**, on Twitter/X at **@Summersdale** and on Instagram and TikTok at **@summersdalebooks** and get in touch.
We'd love to hear from you!

www.summersdale.com